Identity Recycling

Identity Recycling

Ana Gomes

Published by The Invisible Imprint in the United Kingdom in 2023

ISBN: 978-1-83919-521-1

Para a minha irmã Maria e a minha mãe Dialina por nunca desistirem de mim e por incansavelmente me apoiarem durante os tempos mais difíceis. Elas são o significado de força e amor para mim.

Obrigada ao meu pai por sempre me ter apoiado e encorajado a escrever mais e mais.

A woman must have money and a room of her own if she is to write fiction.

- Virginia Woolf, *A Room of One's Own*

Identity Recycling

I saw my face in the screen reflection
Was it me I saw or a past version
Pronounced cheekbones, a tilted nose to the
right, a curved upper lip stuck in disapproval
How long does it take, how much of life do
we have to live, until our face is unrecognisa-
ble to ourselves
We mark time in our clocks but our body
marks life years

Who am I?
She from the past told me…
You were born from the universal bank of
babies
A little mix of recycled energy bundled in a
body
What you make out of it is yours only

Who am I?

She from the future told me…
You have been deposited into the universal
bank of corpses
A little gift of energy for the earth to recycle
and reuse
That is the inevitability of the universe

And so I shout from the mountain
Remember me tomorrow

And so begging, I ask the river
Take me with you forever

And so tonight I embrace the wind, and
dance

Captivity/The Fear

It's strained, like an old violin that hasn't
been touched in a decade
Strings of leather cannot be played

Self-imposed limits on action
Is it the nature or the deceit of the mind
That prevents the freedom I procure

To be bound looks so good
On others' souls
I don't want to be a slave
To the world

Let me go
Protect my freedom
With your life
Let me go

I disappear beneath the dark earth

One and the same
We control plants for our benefit
We control animals for our benefit
We control humans for our benefit
We control we subdue we tame we educate

Let me go
Protect my freedom
With your life
Let me go

Heroine

The rhythm of a heroine

Can you feel the love
In everything she does
For you

There ain't a greater sacrifice
Than to give your life to your child
And it goes unnoticed, unrecognised
Like it's a natural obligation

Ungrateful bastard there's no such thing
(as a natural obligation)
She gave you her life
She's the reason humankind survives

And I'm grateful
So grateful
For everything you've done for me

You moulded me
From a flat piece of clay
You made me a piece of art

And I only hope one day
I'll repay the debt of love I've incurred
And I wonder whether
This is how humankind survives

Thank you, I will live on for you

Triumphant Beetle

Triumphant beetle
Tests my patience
Respect us a little
And this ambience

The dignified
Alone in their palaces
How does one justify
The fear in their traces

Have they ever felt
Something greater than themselves
The ego controlling has dealt
The books in shelves
Too tall to reach

Admit defeat
There is no cure to loneliness

Unless in the way we meet
Each time we undress
Come back to me
For you I am yearning
There is no peace in waiting
For the moment I can feel thee

Logical Nonsense

Breaking the glass
Laughing too long after the joke
Tripping over the incoherence on the pave-
ment

Social suicide
It's Entertainment

There is no life of disguise
I am what you see and who you think I am
If you are in love with mystery.
Then solve a crime don't force love upon me

Self-prophecy determines action and inaction
amongst us
To know what another envisions is intimacy

Process your madness
Judge its depth before professing it

Determining truth can be unattainable
We are all schizophrenics at best
And normal at worst

At least there is one truth
Respiring cells
I am alive and at the majesty's service

Looming

The illness lottery
Who's it going to curse next?
The school friend, the neighbour's cat, the
mother's daughter, the unborn child
You or me

Bring me the weapon
I'll do it myself
There's gonna be no rotting
Inside of me

Gnawing from the inside out
Debilitating the best of us
Are you a parasite or a friend?

Grow grow grow grow
Take everything I have
Take my rest take my peace take my painless
reverie

They say meditate
I tell them
Hypnotize me
I want out of here
Release me
I'm a prisoner to my body

What ends will we go to be free
And will my mind ever forgive me
If I somehow choose
Wrong

Woman

The problem is that
I feel like a woman with you
And that defeats the point doesn't it
It's not the only thing I am

Pain

My brain is a frazzled pot
And I don't know what to do with it
I feel cold coming from the inside
It's like an arctic inside
It spread out and it hurts
It physically hurts
The ice caps are breaking through my bones
I need the sun but we are in winter and it
will not come

I used to have a passion for life
I think that's been robbed away from me

I am in a house in Porto
I grew up here from when I was seventeen or
so
I am trying to make sense of what's hap-
pened to me

My mother used to say "chronic stress is bad
for your health"
I thought I was invincible
I convinced myself so

Brain Fog

My brain feels battered.

I was reduced to a corner of my own mind.

Pressured against my own skull.

Words and language have so much power.
They can dissuade as much as they can per-
suade. They can infiltrate your subconscious
through repetition. You might even start to
think they are your own words. Horrible
words used to hurt your worth and your es-
teem.

It was over a year of this. At the end I had
lost my words. I would eat so I didn't have to
speak. That way my words couldn't be used
against me.

The downfall was so significant. How did no
one see it coming? How did no one stop it?

Social isolation is a crime against humanity. It strips you of the backbone of you. My body and brain no longer connected to my soul. They were militant. Serving someone else's purpose but mine. I discovered you can be dead and breathing at the same time.

I was made to believe whatever suited. I was told what to think, how to think, the right way to think. How to listen to music, how to be close with your friends, how to cook, how to eat. From a full-grown woman I became a puppet to their desires, their dreams, their wants. Or else his desires, his dreams, his wants.

Abuse is a craft. It's delivered systematically and subtly so you feel like a fool. He created insecurities where there were none. He set up traps with compliments and gathered infor-mation. Collecting and collating, classifying

my insecurities in an orderly fashion for ease
of recollection when delivering a punch.
Then he created them.

There was horror in it. Disguised as it was, it
was not completely concealed.

And I will never be the same.

Piano Man

The piano makes me feel sad now
We did not know how to care for our love
Despite this
I feel a strong desire to embrace you today
I'm not sure why or how but you are haunt-
ing me
Is it in the air of London
That air we once shared?
Or are you thinking of me too?
I have been on the verge of tears all day
Even the pills cannot erase those tears away
When you know you have loved deeply
And you are only at the ripe age of twenty-
four
I am in mourning for our love

He smoked reality away after work,
He had a pack of sleeping pills in his drug
box (our laundry box).

I tried dancing it away one night,
But it wasn't enough to set me free.
We did not make love anymore.
He lay down in the couch with his instant gratification,
Twitter and audiobooks became the everyday norm.
I perched in the corner or sat uncomfortable in a hard table chair,
Staring at him,
Wondering where he's gone.
We had a house: four walls a door and a ceiling.
But we never made a home.

Unhealthy Love

I want you to live your life without a single fear in your heart.

And I want you to know you have my spirit there facing it with you wherever there may be.

And I want you to feel my love as an injection of life into your mortal body.

And I want you to have no doubt in your heart that I'm yours because I know I'll be yours for the rest of this moment.

And I hope that somehow that takes some of your fear away.

Ana Gomes is a Portuguese London-based writer who is passionate about her family, her culture and roots as well as striving for freedom and experimentation. She studied at Imperial College London to become a doctor and is currently working for the NHS. She started writing when she was young and became more prolific slowly over time.

Ana mostly writes poetry and short stories that aim to capture an emotion or a moment or place, often in nature.

9 781839 195211